W9-AXD-059

CITIES OF THE WORLD

NEW YORK CITY

BY DEBORAH KENT

 CHILDREN'S PRESS®
A Division of Grolier Publishing
New York London Hong Kong Sydney
Danbury, Connecticut

CONSULTANTS

Richard E. Altman, B.S.
Key contributor to the book *New York: Metropolis of the American Dream;*
Former Manager of Communications, New York Convention & Visitors Bureau

Linda Cornwell
Learning Resource Consultant
Indiana Department of Education

Project Editor: Downing Publishing Services
Design Director: Karen Kohn & Associates
Photo Researcher: Jan Izzo

Library of Congress Cataloging-in-Publication Data
Kent, Deborah.
    New York City / by Deborah Kent.
       p. cm. — (Cities of the world)
    Includes index.
    Summary: Describes the history, people, and places of New York City.
    ISBN 0-516-20025-9 (lib. bdg.)   ISBN 0-516-26072-3 (pbk.)
    1. New York City (N.Y.)—Juvenile literature. [1. New York City (N.Y.)]
I. Title. II. Series: Cities of the world (New York, N.Y.)
F128.33.K46   1996   96-19906
974.7'1—dc20   CIP
                                                   AC

TABLE OF CONTENTS

POSSIBLE

August 8, 1974, began like any other day. Thousands of workers streamed into New York's World Trade Center. Suddenly, an extraordinary sight caught their attention. Far overhead, a man walked back and forth on a high wire. The wire stretched between the Trade Center's lofty twin towers.

The towers of the World Trade Center rise 1,350 feet, nearly a quarter of a mile, into the sky. The crowd that gathered in the Trade Center plaza that August morning gazed upward in amazement. The unknown high-wire artist danced and leaped. He lay down on the wire and rolled from side to side. People clapped and cheered. "Who would believe it!" they exclaimed to one another. "This could happen only in New York!"

The police took a dimmer view. They placed the daredevil, a young man from France named Phillippe Petit, under arrest. Petit was charged with trespassing and taken before a judge. The judge handed down an unusual sentence. He ordered Petit to give a free performance in the city's Central Park. Petit had done no harm to anyone with his stunt. Now, New York's children would enjoy his daring and skill.

New York is a city of islands and waterways, tunnels and bridges. It has five sections, or boroughs: Manhattan, Brooklyn, Queens, Staten Island, and the Bronx. Each of the boroughs could be a city in its own right.

In the summer of 1974, high-wire artist Phillipe Petit (right) walked across a high wire between the twin towers of the World Trade Center (above).

The Midtown Manhattan skyline can be seen in the background, beyond the East River and the Queensboro Bridge.

Each tower of the World Trade Center has an observation deck on the 110th floor. From this height, there is a splendid view of the city. It includes the glass-and-steel towers of Midtown Manhattan and the rolling hills of Staten Island. To the east, across the East River, lie the densely packed houses of Brooklyn and Queens. To the north sprawls the Bronx, the only borough that is part of the mainland.

New York is by far the biggest city in the United States. It has twice as many people as Los Angeles, the nation's second largest city. New York leads the country in theater and the fine arts. It is one of the world's vital centers of business and finance. Yet the city's greatest asset is its people. They come from immensely diverse backgrounds and have an endless array of talents. And there are so many of them!

New York is a startling city. At times, it can be overwhelming. It may inspire love or hate, but seldom a feeling of indifference. One fact is plain. Somehow things happen here that don't occur anywhere else. In New York City, all things are possible.

In 1906, writer O. Henry published a collection of short stories called *The Four Million*. The title referred to the 4 million people who lived in New York City at that time. O. Henry felt that each person in the city was a unique individual with a story to tell.

Today, the population of New York City has swelled to more than 7 million. Its people trace their roots to every continent on the globe. The city has a special way of shaping and molding its inhabitants. Whether their ancestors came from Ireland, Sicily, or West Africa, they are New Yorkers, all 7 million of them. Each one has a story worth telling.

THE CITY OF PROMISES

Ever since its founding in 1625, New York has been a magnet for people from other lands. The first immigrants were Europeans who arrived during the 1600s. Most came from the Netherlands and Great Britain. Yet, because New York was an important seaport, it drew people from many other countries as well. This trend has continued throughout the city's long history. Today, it is often said that New York and its suburbs have more Greeks than Athens, more Poles than Warsaw, more Jews than Tel Aviv, and more Italians than Rome.

Above: This child's face has been painted for the Caribbean Day parade in Brooklyn.

Right: Boys playing with car tires on a New York street

People of African descent comprise New York's largest ethnic group. About 2.1 million black people live here, more than in any other American city. After World War II, thousands of African Americans poured into New York from the rural South. Most sought jobs in the city's factories. More recently, people of African heritage have also come from Jamaica, Trinidad, Haiti, and other islands in the Caribbean.

African Americans make up the largest ethnic group in New York City. The woman above is a firefighter. The Jamaican family shown on the right owns a shoe-repair business in Brooklyn.

About 15 percent of all New Yorkers are Jewish. Jewish immigrants came to the city from Germany, Poland, Russia, and many other countries. People of Italian, Chinese, Irish, German, and Russian ancestry are also well represented in the city. Hispanics make up about 12 percent of New York's population. The majority are Puerto Ricans. Other Hispanic people have come from the Dominican Republic, Mexico, and Central America.

More newcomers pour into New York every day. On any busy street, you might see a woman dressed in a Japanese kimono or an Indian sari. You can buy a candy bar from a man from Pakistan or hail a cab whose driver came from Nigeria. New York is the port of entry for people from all over the world. For many, it becomes a permanent home.

People from other lands usually come to New York in search of better opportunities. Through hard work, they hope to earn money and build a rewarding future.

For many native-born Americans, New York holds out the same shining

This Polish family lives in Brooklyn. It is often said that New York and its suburbs have more Poles than Warsaw.

Left: An Indian woman in a sari attends
a festival in New York City.
Above: A Brooklyn rabbi reads the Torah
with Hebrew school students.

promise. The city lures young women and men from the nearby suburbs, from southern towns, and from midwestern cities. Some dream of becoming painters, writers, dancers, or actors. Others hope to grow rich in the world of high finance.

Many newcomers don't care what sort of job pays their rent. They simply want to live in New York. They are enthralled by its museums, plays, and concerts. Its tiny shops and huge department stores fill them with wonder. These people never tire of exploring the side streets and discovering the neighborhoods that give New York a character all its own.

A CITY OF NEIGHBORHOODS

The signs along Manhattan's Mott Street are printed in both English letters and Chinese characters. Shops sell gingerroot, black mushrooms, and bamboo shoots. Many telephone booths have pointed roofs like Chinese pagodas. Mott Street runs through the heart of New York's Chinatown. Chinatown is immensely popular with tourists, who flock to its restaurants. They love to sample such exotic dishes as chicken with peanuts, shrimp with lobster sauce, and Peking duck. But for thousands of Chinese immigrants, Chinatown is a home away from home. In the security of familiar customs, they learn the ways of their adopted land. Like the Chinese, nearly every immigrant group has founded its own community in New York. By gathering in these special enclaves, people preserve the customs and languages of the old country. Ethnic communities are like villages in the middle of the city. People know one another by

Left: Participants in a Queens Korean festival
Below: Food vendors in Chinatown

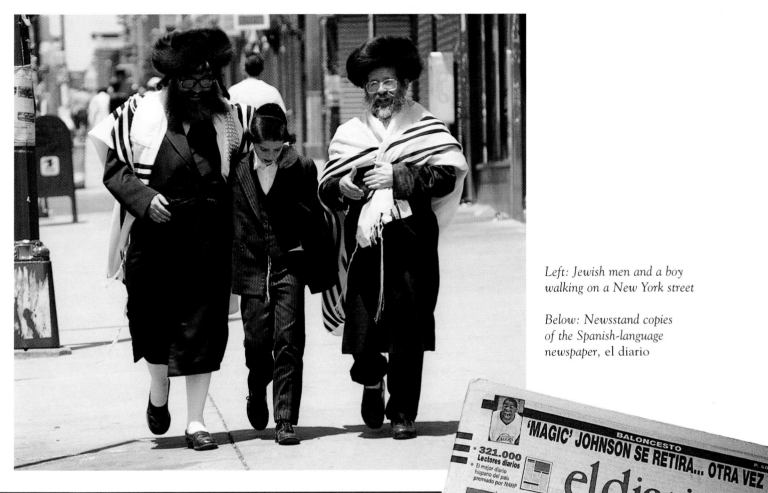

Left: Jewish men and a boy walking on a New York street

Below: Newsstand copies of the Spanish-language newspaper, el diario

name. Neighbors help one another in times of sickness or death. The elderly try to pass traditions to the younger generation.

On Manhattan's Lower East Side, families from Puerto Rico shop in tiny grocery stores called *bodegas*. The most popular newspaper is *el diario*, a Spanish-language daily.

In Brooklyn's Crown Heights section, a community of Hasidic Jews flourishes. The Hasids are an orthodox sect whose men wear long curls called earlocks that hang in front of their ears. Other neighborhoods in New York are magnets for people from Poland, Italy, India, or Vietnam.

African Americans from the South have also formed communities in New York. The oldest of these is Harlem, in Manhattan. Much of Harlem is riddled with poverty. But the neighborhood has prosperous sections as well. During the 1920s and 1930s, Harlem attracted leading African American writers, artists, and musicians. This period is known as the Harlem Renaissance.

Not all of New York's neighborhoods have an ethnic flavor. Greenwich Village in Manhattan has long been a haven for would-be writers, artists, and actors.

Teenage girls in Brooklyn

Many painters and sculptors display their work in Village galleries. Other artists prefer Soho, a neighboring district of former warehouses. With their vast floor space, high ceilings, and oversized windows, warehouses make excellent artists' studios.

Life in New York isn't for everyone. It can be hectic, frustrating, and even frightening. But despite the drawbacks, more than 7 million people make the city their home. They adapt to its demands and thrive on its excitement.

Washington Square Park in Greenwich Village, with its Memorial Arch (above), draws crowds of people who are often entertained by street musicians (right).

LIVING IN THE BIG APPLE

"Just remember," runs a popular New York saying, "you're nothing but a worm in the Big Apple." The "Big Apple" is a nickname for New York City. New York can be overwhelming. At times, it makes the most seasoned native feel helpless.

When most people think of New York, they picture Manhattan. In area, Manhattan is actually the smallest of the five boroughs. It is a long, narrow island, covering only 34 square miles. One and a half million people live packed together on this speck of land. Single-family homes hardly exist. Most people live in small apartments. Even so, housing is in short supply. Rents in Manhattan are the highest in the country.

A view of the "Big Apple" from Brooklyn

Some of the wealthiest people in the world live in elegant Manhattan apartment buildingss like the one pictured above. Other New York City residents live in areas such as Brownsville (left), one of the poorest communities in the country.

Midtown and Lower Manhattan bristle with skyscrapers. In the other boroughs, most buildings are lower. Staten Island, Brooklyn, Queens, and the Bronx have many private homes as well as apartments. Brooklyn is known for its row houses, side-by-side houses that adjoin one another.

Some of the wealthiest people in the world have apartments in Manhattan's elegant high-rises. Yet New York also has neighborhoods blighted by poverty. Brownsville in Brooklyn and sections of the South Bronx are among the poorest communities in the nation. Families jam together in tiny apartments. Homeless people sleep in doorways, or build houses of cardboard boxes. Gangs prowl the streets, selling drugs and fighting for territory.

Out-of-towners often think of New York as the nation's crime capital. Actually, statistics do not support this reputation. In 1994, FBI crime figures ranked New York only 42nd among the nation's 50 largest cities. In other words, 41 American cities reported higher crime rates than did New York. But muggings, burglaries, and even murders are still tragically frequent in New York. Most New Yorkers pride themselves on being "streetwise." They learn to avoid trouble by walking quickly and purposefully along well-lighted streets. Many guard their windows with bars and grates, and lock their doors with triple bolts.

These people were among the millions of Americans who celebrated the 100th birthday of the Statue of Liberty during the 1986 Fourth of July weekend.

Sunday Bargains

Every Sunday, thousands of eager shoppers crowd Orchard Street on Manhattan's Lower East Side. Along the sidewalks, vendors sell clothing, belts, and purses. Bargaining is not only allowed but encouraged. Orchard Street arose as an outdoor market early in the twentieth century, when the Lower East Side was a neighborhood of Jewish immigrants.

New York is sometimes called the "city that never sleeps." Many supermarkets, ice cream parlors, and dry cleaners stay open all night long. Taxis cruise the streets around the clock. Buses and subways run 24 hours a day. Visitors often complain that the subways are dirty, noisy, and overcrowded. Most New Yorkers accept these conditions as a fact of life. The subway tunnels form a sprawling underground network. They link all the boroughs except Staten Island. The subways take people where they want to go. And New Yorkers are on the move night and day.

Visitors—and even many New Yorkers—enjoy touring the "city that never sleeps" in double-decker buses like this one.

HARBOR

In 1625, a Dutch official named Peter Minuit made one of history's most remarkable purchases. He bought the island of Manhattan from a group of Algonquian Indians. In payment, the Algonquians received a heap of knives, kettles, and beads worth about 40 dollars. Manhattan is now the pulsing center of the biggest city in the nation. But some people despise its rush and confusion. They claim that the Algonquians got the better end of the deal.

LIFE ON THE FRONTIER

During the sixteenth and seventeenth centuries, European rulers grabbed up chunks of the New World. In 1609, the king of the Netherlands (Holland), hired an English captain named Henry Hudson. The Dutch king ordered Hudson to explore a portion of the North American coast. Hudson discovered a broad bay that would make a fine harbor. Sailing into the bay, he found the mouth of the river that now bears his name. Hudson claimed the river, the bay, and the land around them for the Netherlands. New Netherland included parts of present-day New York, New Jersey, and Connecticut.

The Dutch soon established New Amsterdam, a tiny outpost on the southern tip of Manhattan. The name *Manhattan* comes from an Algonquian word meaning "Island of the Hills." The island was indeed hilly and rocky. It had thick woods, clear springs, and small natural caves. Game was plentiful, and there was excellent

Above: New Amsterdam as it looked in 1659

Left: Unpopular Dutch governor Peter Stuyvesant (with cane) surrendered New Amsterdam to the British in 1664.

By 1667, New York Harbor had helped make the city a leading trade center for Britain's American colonies.

fishing. But the Dutch settlement was hardly a paradise. Native Americans sometimes attacked the village. The colonists quarreled among themselves. Their stern governor, Peter Stuyvesant, was unpopular. As in most New World colonies at that time, African slaves were bought and sold.

In 1664, British warships sailed into the harbor at New Amsterdam. The colonists were eager to end Peter Stuyvesant's rule. The Dutch made little resistance to the invasion. The British captured the settlement easily. They renamed it New York, in honor of the king's brother James, the Duke of York.

Under the British, New York grew steadily. To defend themselves against Indian attack, the colonists built a wall of upright stakes across the lower tip of Manhattan. Years later, a street was laid out where the wall once stood. It was named Wall Street. Today, Wall Street is the financial capital of the world.

New York Harbor bristled with masts. Vessels unloaded bundles of cloth, barrels of nails, and chests of tea. New York was a trade center for Britain's American colonies. As time passed, however, the colonists became discontent under British rule. New York soon became a leader in a revolution.

GROWING WITH A NEW NATION

War erupted between Britain and the colonies in 1775. The following year, British forces landed on Manhattan. New York was defended by General George Washington and his Continental army. After a series of bloody skirmishes, the British drove Washington across the Hudson. The port of New York was in British hands.

The British held New York for the next seven years. Red-coated British soldiers patrolled the streets. New Yorkers were forced to quarter British officers in their homes. Sometimes, the officers held grand balls or put on plays. Some colonists felt that the British improved the quality of life in the city. Others, however, complained that the British seized the best produce in the markets. New Yorkers were left with day-old bread and wilted vegetables, all for inflated prices.

In 1783, the war ended with the Treaty of Paris. The colonies were free to form a new nation, the United States of America. George Washington returned to New York in triumph. He held a special victory dinner at Fraunces Tavern, a popular Manhattan gathering place. During 1785,

In 1783, George Washington returned to New York as the leader of a victorious American army.

New York became the nation's temporary capital. George Washington was inaugurated as president on the balcony of Manhattan's Federal Hall in 1789.

Most of New York's population was still concentrated at the lower end of Manhattan. But several neighboring villages were growing in importance. One was Harlem, founded by the Dutch in 1658 near

Manhattan's northern tip. The Bronx sprang up around the farm of Jonas Bronk. The village of Brooklyn, at the western end of Long Island, was incorporated in 1816.

By 1820, 120,000 people lived in New York. It was the largest city in the United States. At the time, the name *New York City* referred only to Manhattan. The neighbor-

ing villages remained independent. Then, in 1898, five distinct communities merged under one centralized government. New York became a sprawling metropolis with five boroughs: Manhattan, the Bronx, Brooklyn, Queens, and Staten Island. Each was unique. Through the twentieth century, they struggled to meet new challenges together.

In 1789, George Washington was inaugurated president of the United States (above). By 1831, New York was the largest city in the country. The engraving on the left shows the old Broadway stagecoaches in 1831.

COME ONE, COME ALL!

Ellis Island is a tiny outcropping of rock in New York Harbor. In 1892, Ellis Island opened as a processing station for newly arrived immigrants to the United States. Its Great Hall was a babble of languages: Italian, Russian, Yiddish, German, Greek. Frightened and weary, families clung together. No one knew what to expect from this strange new land. Brusque officials demanded to know where they had come from and where they intended to go. Doctors probed ears and eyes for any sign of disability or disease. Anyone deemed unfit for life in America was rejected and sent home on the next ship.

Despite the rigors of Ellis Island, New York stretched out a generous hand. As they sailed into New York Harbor, newcomers saw the statue of a woman with an upraised torch. It was the beloved Statue of Liberty. The inscription on its base was a welcome to all:

New arrivals at Ellis Island line up to have their papers examined.

Give me your tired, your poor,

Your huddled masses yearning to breathe free,

The wretched refuse of your teeming shore,

Send these, the homeless, tempest-tossed, to me:

I lift my lamp beside the golden door.

Between 1892 and 1954, 16 million immigrants passed through Ellis Island. Many settled in New York City. They lived in crowded, run-down buildings called tenements. Children and adults alike worked 12- and 14-hour shifts in the city's factories. Some people were defeated by the dreariness of this new life. Many eventually found better jobs. They saved money, educated their children, and left the slums behind. When they moved on, they were replaced by the next generation of newcomers.

The entrance to Ellis Island, which was renovated and reopened in 1991

New York's Little Flower

During his twelve years in office (1932-1946), Mayor Fiorello LaGuardia broke the corrupt political machine that had controlled New York City for more than a century. LaGuardia's father was Italian, and his mother was Jewish. The Italian name *Fiorello* means "little flower." LaGuardia won the love and support of the city's immigrant population. New Yorkers still remember his warmth and humor. During a newspaper strike, LaGuardia read the comic strips over the radio so no one would have to miss them.

Slowly, the five boroughs knitted themselves into a city. The Brooklyn Bridge forged the first link when it joined Brooklyn and Manhattan in 1883. In 1936, the Triborough Bridge connected Manhattan with Queens and the Bronx. The Verrazano Narrows Bridge, finished in 1964, joined Brooklyn and Staten Island. Beneath the city streets sprawled the subway system, with 469 stations along 720 miles of track.

During the twentieth century, New York skyscrapers rose higher and higher. In 1913, the 792-foot Woolworth Building became the tallest human-made structure in the world. In 1931, it was overshadowed by the Empire State Building, which soared 102 stories above the streets. For more than 40 years, the Empire State Building reigned as the tallest in the world. Then, in 1973, it was outdone by the 110-story towers of the World Trade Center. The Trade Center lost its title in 1974, when the Sears Tower was completed in Chicago.

The Eighth Wonder of the World

Soon after work got underway on construction of the Brooklyn Bridge, Washington Roebling, the chief engineer, was badly injured on the job. For the next ten years, Roebling oversaw the work from his bed. He monitored progress from the window of his apartment, watching through a telescope. With a central span of 1,595 feet, the Brooklyn Bridge was the longest suspension bridge that had ever been built. It was sometimes called the "Eighth Wonder of the World."

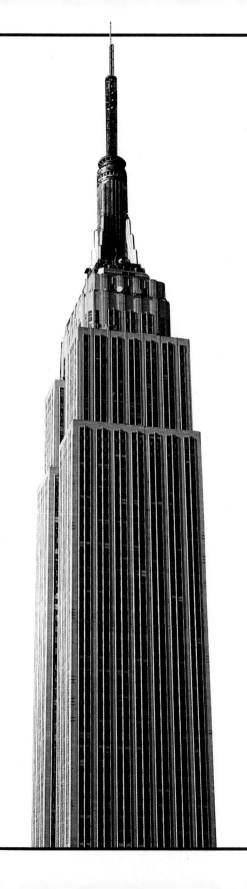

Throughout most of its history, New York has been unrivaled as America's biggest city. In population, it is larger than 41 of the 50 states. The city has more than 900 public schools. Its sanitation crews haul away 23,000 tons of garbage a day. New York has all of the problems that trouble other American cities: drugs, crime, and poverty. But because of its size, it has them on a grander scale. Yet, while public officials argue about solutions, the people of New York go on with their lives. They study, work, and play as people always have in this complex, extraordinary city.

Above: Huge crowds mob Fifth Avenue in New York, the biggest city in the United States.

Left: The Empire State Building

An egg cream is a frothy milkshake concoction sold at many New York lunch counters. It is usually made with milk, soda water, and chocolate syrup. The original egg cream was thickened with an egg. It was invented on Manhattan's Lower East Side early in the twentieth century. Egg creams are among the countless pleasures unique to the town that is sometimes called Fun City.

NEW YORKERS AT PLAY

Winter in New York can be long and dreary. With the coming of spring, New Yorkers emerge from a kind of hibernation. Children mark the sidewalks with chalk to play marbles and hopscotch. Jump ropes twirl to chants passed down from one generation to the next. Some jump-rope rhymes are native to New York:

> My mother and your mother live across the way:
> Three sixteen, East Broadway . . .
>
> or
>
> No, you can't go to Macy's any more, more, more!
> There's a big fat policeman at the door, door, door!
> He'll make you pay a dollar,
> Or he'll pinch you till you holler,
> So you can't go to Macy's any more, more, more!

Cross-country skiing in Central Park

On the city streets, some children play a game called stickball. Stickball is a form of baseball adapted to crowded urban conditions. The rules may vary from block to block. Anything can serve as a base—a parking meter, a garbage can, or a fire hydrant. A broomstick or mop handle is used for a bat. Needless to say, a ball through a neighbor's window means a run home, not a home run!

Few New York apartment-dwellers have the luxury of a backyard. But this does not keep them from planting flowers. Window boxes blossom with geraniums and petunias. Roses and tulips bloom in pots on terraces. Many people plant roof gardens. In the fall, they harvest tomatoes and zucchinis 20 stories above the street.

Young girl drawing with sidewalk chalk

The people of Manhattan share one common backyard—Central Park. The park is an enormous oblong of grass and trees, hills and lakes. It stretches for 2.5 miles down the middle of the island. Anyone can use the park's tennis courts and softball fields. For a row on the lake, there are boats to rent. For those who prefer less energetic pastimes, the park offers concrete tables inlaid with tile chess squares.

Spectator sports thrill New Yorkers. Baseball's Babe Ruth was the king of New York in the 1920s and 1930s. In the 1990s, basketball's Patrick Ewing was idolized. Teams are honored institutions. The baseball Mets came to New York in 1962. After seven dismal years, they stunned all of baseball by winning the World Series in 1969. New Yorkers danced in the streets.

Left: Babe Ruth, the "King of Swat," in the 1920s

Right: T-Ball in Central Park in the 1990s

Chess players in Central Park

No team in baseball history has won more World Series championships than the New York Yankees. The Yankees, who are based in the Bronx, are proudly known as the Bronx Bombers. For a true Brooklynite, the favorite team is a ghost. From 1913 to 1957, the Brooklyn Dodgers played at cozy Ebbetts Field in the heart of the borough. In 1947, the Dodgers had the courage to sign Jackie Robinson as the first black player in the major leagues. Old-time Brooklynites still claim that some of the life left their community when the Dodgers moved to Los Angeles.

In addition to baseball, New York has several other professional teams. New York's football fans follow the Jets and the Giants. Actually, neither of these teams plays in New York. Their home fields are at the Meadowlands Sports Complex in New Jersey. In recent years, hockey has grown increasingly popular. Fans cheer for the New York Rangers. The New York Knicks play basketball at Madison Square Garden. The "Garden" is also used for boxing matches, athletic exhibitions, and such nonsports events as concerts and the circus.

Sports are only one form of entertainment enjoyed by New Yorkers. In music, dance, and theater, New York is renowned throughout the world.

Those who paddle rowboats on Central Park's lake enjoy a calm and beautiful setting in the midst of a bustling city.

CURTAIN TIME!

Give my regards to Broadway,

Remember me to Herald Square!

Tell all the boys on Forty-second Street

That I will soon be there!

This old song refers to the famous avenue that makes New York the theater capital of the world. Broadway theaters are especially noted for musicals. Many theater buffs claim that Broadway reached its peak during the 1940s and 1950s. At that time, theatergoers lined up for tickets to such classics as *Oklahoma!* and *South Pacific.* In later years, *The Sound of Music* and *My Fair Lady* were long-running hits. Songs from those shows are woven into American culture. Broadway continues to produce hit shows today. Some people complain that the new tunes are unsingable and the lyrics lack spirit. Nevertheless, many shows are sold out months in advance.

Broadway shows usually have large casts, complex staging, and elaborate costumes. They are very expensive to produce. More streamlined productions can be seen at New York's "off Broadway" and "off-off-Broadway" theaters. These theaters often put on new material by unknown playwrights. They provide opportunities for hundreds of aspiring actors. But for actors and playwrights alike, the lights of Broadway continue to beckon.

Each year, opera fans from around the world flock to the "Met." The "Met" is their affectionate nickname for the Metropolitan Opera House at Manhattan's Lincoln Center for the Performing Arts. During the summer, the Met hosts the American Ballet Theater. Lincoln Center's concert facilities include Avery Fisher Hall and Alice Tully Hall.

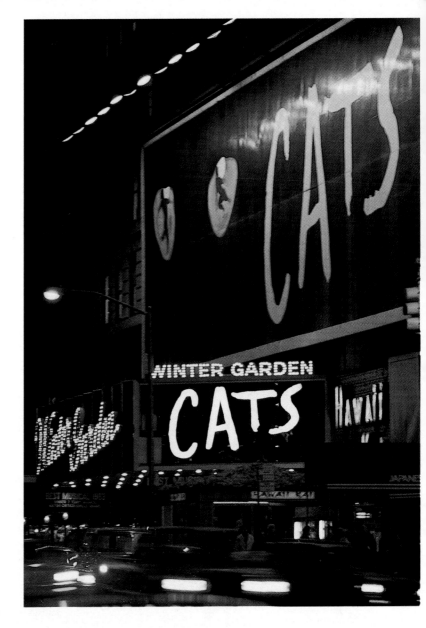

The Winter Garden hosted the long-running musical Cats.

"How do you get to Carnegie Hall?" a tourist asked a New Yorker on the street. The New Yorker shrugged and answered, "Practice, practice!" Carnegie Hall is New York's foremost concert auditorium. The world's finest classical and popular musicians perform there. The chance to play at Carnegie Hall marks the pinnacle of a musician's career.

Ticket prices for plays and concerts in New York can be discouragingly steep. But no one in the city need live without culture. Every summer, New Yorkers can choose from a vast array of free plays and concerts in the city parks. Sitting on a blanket under the stars, New Yorkers can hear a Beethoven symphony, a jazz

trio, or a rock band. Open-air theaters offer Shakespeare, children's plays, and puppet shows. Even Broadway shows often offer half-price tickets on the day of a performance.

Outdoor theater is only one form of free entertainment in New York. Throughout the year, the city provides festivals and parades to delight young and old.

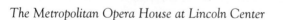

The Metropolitan Opera House at Lincoln Center

PARTIES IN THE STREETS

You don't have to be Irish to enjoy St. Patrick's Day. On March 17, New Yorkers of every ethnic persuasion pour into the streets to honor Ireland's patron saint. A splendid parade of green-clad marchers makes its way down Manhattan's Fifth Avenue. Bands blare out "When Irish Eyes Are Smiling" and "Molly Malone." Everyone yearns for the Emerald Isle. Even those whose forebears came from Russia, Hong Kong, or Puerto Rico are Irish for a day.

You don't have to be Italian to honor San Gennaro, the patron saint of Naples, Italy. The Feast of San Gennaro is held in Manhattan's Little Italy section each September. People throng the streets, which are closed to traffic. Games of chance and skill are set up in booths along the sidewalks. A lucky toss of a ring over a peg can win a goldfish, a beaded necklace, or a giant teddy bear. In the heat of Indian summer, it's impossible to pass up Italian ices. Rich cream-filled pastries called *cannoli* and long, crusty loaves of fresh bread are tempting delights. A roller coaster, Ferris wheel, and other rides thrill the adventurous.

Daily specials are listed on this sidewalk menu in New York City's Little Italy.

This group is enjoying New York's St. Patrick's Day Parade.

Erin go Bragh

Fun for the Whole Family

People sometimes complain that New York is a cold place where neighbors don't care about one another. But when they hold block parties, neighbors get together for friendship and fun. The street is closed to traffic and open to music, dancing, food, and games.

You don't have to be Chinese to celebrate the Chinese New Year. The Chinese lunar calendar is based on the phases of the moon. By its reckoning, the new year begins in late January or early February. Colorful banners float above the streets of Chinatown. Vendors sell pastries filled with lotus seeds, nuts, and raisins. The height of the celebration is a grand parade with dragon dancers. A magnificent fireworks display lights up the night sky.

You don't even have to be a New Yorker to enjoy the Macy's Thanksgiving Day Parade. Every year on Thanksgiving morning, this New York extravaganza is televised across the country. The parade, sponsored by Macy's Department Store, was made famous by the classic movie *Miracle on 34th Street.* Spectacular

The Dragon Dance is the highlight of the Chinatown New Year's Day Parade.

Gigantic helium balloons like these are a big part of the Macy's Thanksgiving Day Parade.

helium balloons dance in the sky. They are shaped like animals, fruits and vegetables, and cartoon characters. Dozens of schools, stores, and neighborhoods have floats in the parade. One float always carries Santa Claus in an enormous sleigh. For families across America, the Macy's Santa ushers in the Christmas season each year.

"East side, west side, all around the town," begins the old song called "The Sidewalks of New York." New York is so big that you could spend a lifetime learning your way all around it. Each of the five boroughs offers unique treats and surprises.

BROOKLYN AND QUEENS

Brooklyn and Queens occupy the western tip of Long Island. The East River separates them from Manhattan. Brooklyn has some 2.5 million people, more than any other borough. If Brooklyn were a city in its own right, it would be the fourth largest in the United States.

The Brooklyn Historical Society displays many prized relics of the borough's past. Among them are bats and balls once used by the Brooklyn Dodgers. An extensive library preserves books and photographs that tell the story of Brooklyn people and places.

Prospect Park is a 536-acre playground for city dwellers. It is a lovely blend of woodlands, streams, and meadows. The park's Picnic House hosts plays, dance performances, concerts, and other events year-round. A 60-acre lake is home to a noisy flock of ducks and swans. Picnickers soon discover that the birds aren't shy about begging for handouts.

The Brooklyn Museum is one of the finest art museums in the United States. Its collections include ancient Egyptian stone carvings, paintings by American artists, and a sculpture garden.

On the southern edge of Brooklyn is Coney Island, one of New York's favorite summer spots. The Cyclone, Coney Island's old-fashioned wooden roller coaster, is world-famous. Thrill seekers consider it one of the wildest rides on earth. Less daring souls can

The Japanese Garden in Brooklyn Botanic Garden is a lovely place to rest and appreciate the beautifully landscaped grounds.

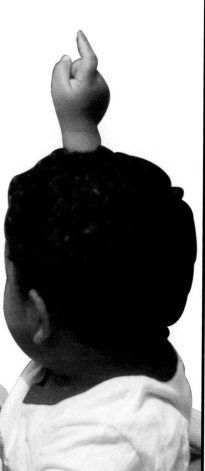

Brooklyn. Though it is part of the city, Queens has a suburban feel. Most people live in small apartment buildings or single-family homes with pleasant backyards. Children in-line skate and ride bikes along quiet, tree-lined side streets.

For millions of people each year, Queens is the first stop on a trip to New York. Both LaGuardia and Kennedy Airports are located here.

Flushing Meadows in Queens was the site of world's fairs in 1939 and 1964. The Unisphere, a 380-ton steel globe, still stands as a relic of the World's Fair of 1964. The nearby Queens Museum houses the Panorama, an elaborate model of the five boroughs. Larger than a football field, the Panorama is so detailed that every street and building in the city can be seen.

New York, the city of skyscrapers, is also home to the largest urban nature preserve in the world. The Jamaica Bay Wildlife Refuge is only a subway ride from Midtown Manhattan. In the shadow of Kennedy Airport, muskrats dive and herons and egrets build their nests.

stroll 3 miles of boardwalk along the beach. Vendors peddle cotton candy, popcorn, and toy monkeys on sticks. The Coney Island Aquarium features sharks, octopuses, and other creatures from the world's oceans.

In area, Queens is the largest of the five boroughs. During the 1960s and 1970s, the population swelled with refugees from overcrowded neighborhoods in Manhattan, the Bronx, and

Children enjoying a Coney Island ride

THE BRONX AND STATEN ISLAND

In the 1600s, a wealthy Dutch farmer named Jonas Bronk owned a large estate on the mainland north of Manhattan. According to legend, he loved to throw parties. People would say, "Let's go up to the Bronks'!" Whether or not this story is true, the word *the* nearly always precedes the name of this northern-most borough.

Bronx Park is the most extensive recreation area in the Bronx. The park embraces the New York Botanical Garden, founded in 1891. The garden's 40-acre forest is the only uncut woodland that survives in New York City. The Conservatory is a greenhouse that displays plants from rain forest and desert habitats.

More than 675 species of animals from around the world can be seen at the Bronx Zoo. The zoo's innovative exhibits include a walk-through rain forest with waterfalls, orchids, and writhing pythons. In another section, a monorail carries visitors past free-roaming antelope, rhinos, and elephants.

Far left: A mother and daughter at the Bronx Zoo

Below: The New York Botanical Garden

The only way to reach Staten Island from Manhattan is by taking the Staten Island Ferry. From 1886 to 1975, a ferry ride cost only five cents. The trip affords a splendid view of Ellis Island, the Statue of Liberty, and Lower Manhattan. Not far from the ferry landing is the Snug Harbor Cultural Center. Several buildings stand on the center's grounds. Concerts and other events are held at the center's Veterans Memorial Hall. The Newhouse Center for Contemporary Art exhibits paintings and sculptures. The Staten Island Children's Museum is noted for its educational hands-on exhibits.

The Staten Island Ferry and the New York skyline at sunset

The Richmondtown Restoration Historical Museum, Staten Island

In area, Staten Island is almost as large as Brooklyn. Yet it has only about 375,000 people, fewer than any of the other four boroughs. Until the 1960s, there were still several working farms on Staten Island. During the 1980s and 1990s, many new housing developments sprang up. Yet Staten Island remains a collection of small towns. With its fields and patches of woods, it does not seem like part of the nation's biggest city.

The Richmondtown Restoration is a reconstructed village on the site of Staten Island's original 1685 settlement. It includes 26 fully restored buildings. Voorlezer's House, built in 1695, is the oldest schoolhouse in the United States. Throughout the village, visitors can watch demonstrations of colonial cooking, spinning, and crafts.

THE HEART OF THE CITY

In 1811, New York City officials decided that all new streets in Manhattan should follow a neat, gridlike pattern. Today, most north-south thoroughfares are numbered and known as avenues. East-west thoroughfares, called streets, are also numbered consecutively. The system makes it very easy for visitors—and residents—to find their way around. But the streets of Lower Manhattan, the oldest part of the city, wander this way and that with no hint of logic. At one point, West Tenth and West Fourth streets intersect.

Manhattan has many distinct sections, each with its own history and character. Harlem, north of 125th Street, has long been a center of the African American community. Many parts of Harlem are wracked with terrible poverty. Church groups, neighborhood associations, and individuals are working hard for improvement. Lovely old buildings have been restored, giving Harlem a new sense of hope.

Manhattan has some of the finest museums in the world. The 234 galleries of the Metropolitan Museum of Art display works from

Throngs of Manhattan office workers crowd the streets during weekday lunch hours.

Watch out for Moving Coats!

Seventh Avenue and 34th Street is the heart of New York's Garment District, where coats and dresses are made and sold. Garment workers push swaying racks of clothing through the streets, causing a constant traffic jam.

every period in history and from every land on earth. A visitor can admire ancient Greek statues, wood carvings from Africa, and Navajo blankets. The museum has room after room of paintings by masters such as Monet and Van Gogh. The Museum of Modern Art includes a unique exhibit on industrial design. As one example, a helicopter hangs in midair above the central escalator.

Above: Spanish Harlem, near the Upper East Side, is the city's largest Spanish-speaking area.

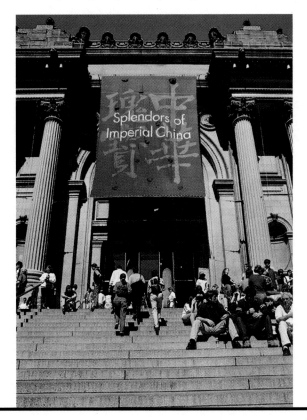

The Metropolitan Museum of Art (left) encourages art students (right) to learn from the masters.

One popular attraction for visitors to Manhattan is Rockefeller Center. This 12-acre complex is a city within the city. It includes stores, restaurants, and office buildings. Its Radio City Music Hall is the world's largest indoor theater, with 5,900 seats. Once used as a movie theater, it now serves as a concert hall. Before special holiday shows, the audience is treated to a show by the Rockettes, a famous troupe of precision dancers. At Christmastime, Rockefeller Plaza

Left: Skaters at Rockefeller Plaza
Below left: Radio City Music Hall, home of the world-famous Rockettes

Below: New York City bus drivers taking a break at Rockefeller Center

becomes an ice rink where skaters circle and glide. Visitors gaze in wonder at a brilliantly lighted Christmas tree that towers 6 stories high.

At the heart of Manhattan is Central Park, the city's major playground. People jeered when the park opened in 1876. Who needed a park in Midtown Manhattan? There were still farms and woodlands all around it. But the park's designers, Frederic Law Olmsted and Calvert Vaux, had a clear vision of the future. As time passed, the city spread to surround the parkland. Today, Central Park is an oasis of green amid a vast desert of concrete.

Central Park's Sheep Meadow, now that the sheep are gone, provides a pleasant place to bask in the sun on a warm summer day. Many New Yorkers use the park as their very own backyard.

New York's financial district is located in Lower Manhattan, the site of the first Dutch settlement. The New York Stock Exchange (NYSE) and the American Stock Exchange (AMEX) on Wall Street are whirlwinds of lightning-fast business deals. Whatever happens on the New York stock exchanges has an impact on the world economy. It is said that when someone sneezes on Wall Street, hats blow off in France.

Whatever happens on the busy floors of New York City's stock exchanges affects markets across the world.

Lady Liberty

The 151-foot figure of *Liberty Enlightening the World* stands at the entrance to New York Harbor. Its upraised torch is a beacon to newcomers. The Statue of Liberty, as it is commonly known, was a gift from France to the United States. It was unveiled in 1886. By climbing 168 spiral stairs, visitors reach the observation platform in the statue's head.

This statue of the "Wall Street Bull" stands in Battery Park.

On the southernmost tip of Manhattan stand the twin towers of the World Trade Center. Anyone in the observation decks at the top can gaze across New York Harbor to Ellis Island, the Statue of Liberty, and Staten Island. Visitors can look north to the skyscrapers of Midtown Manhattan, and beyond the East River to Brooklyn. They might wonder what Peter Minuit would say if he could only see the mighty city that sprang from his tiny village on the island of Manhattan.

FAMOUS LANDMARKS

An exhibit at the Ellis Island Museum

The Statue of Liberty

The Brooklyn Bridge

Cleopatra's Needle, the Central Park obelisk

Brooklyn Bridge
Once the longest suspension bridge in the world. Completed in 1883, the bridge was the first link between Brooklyn and Manhattan. Pedestrians may cross by means of a walkway.

Ellis Island
The processing station for millions of European immigrants from 1892 to 1954. The Great Hall is now open as a museum, telling the story of immigration through photographs and first-hand accounts.

Statue of Liberty
A figure of a woman with an upraised torch. The statue represents Liberty breaking Tyranny's chains. It stands on Liberty Island at the mouth of New York Harbor.

Coney Island
A favorite summer resort for New Yorkers. Coney Island has beaches, boardwalks, an aquarium, and a botanical garden. Its famous roller coaster, the Cyclone, is one of the wildest in the world.

Central Park
A vast rectangle of grass and trees in the middle of Manhattan. Attractions include Central Park Lake, a small zoo, and Cleopatra's Needle, an ancient Egyptian obelisk.

Guggenheim Museum
An unusual white, funnel-shaped building designed by architect Frank Lloyd Wright. The museum has a noted collection of paintings by French Impressionist artists.

Metropolitan Museum of Art
The largest art museum in the United States, covering 4 square blocks. The museum owns some 2 million works of art. Exhibits come from every country on earth and represent every period in history.

Rockefeller Center
A 12-acre complex of stores and office buildings. Among them is Radio City Music Hall, the largest indoor theater in the world, with 5,900 seats. At Christmastime, a spectacular tree stands in the plaza.

The Metropolitan
Museum of Art

One of the dinosaurs
in the popular Jurassic
Park exhibit at New
York City's Museum
of Natural History

One of the two lion
statues in front of
the New York
Public Library

Museum of Natural History
The most extensive natural history museum in the world. Exhibits include dinosaur skeletons, mounted whales, and dioramas showing creatures in an assortment of habitats.

New York Public Library
Landmark building in Midtown Manhattan. The front entrance is guarded by a pair of marble lions called Patience and Fortitude.

Times Square
An area of office buildings and hotels near the Broadway theater district. At the stroke of midnight on December 31, a giant ball drops in Times Square to signal the start of the New Year.

Trinity Church
Rebuilt in 1840 on the site of the original 1698 structure, Trinity Church is a landmark on Wall Street.

St. Patrick's Cathedral
Ornate Gothic cathedral in Midtown Manhattan. It is noted for its stained-glass windows and bronze doors.

Staten Island Ferry
Still one of the least expensive rides in the country, though the nickel fare was abolished in 1975. The trip between Staten Island and Manhattan lasts 20 minutes. It offers a wonderful view of Ellis Island, the Statue of Liberty, and Lower Manhattan.

Jamaica Bay Wildlife Refuge
The largest urban nature preserve in the world. Visitors may explore marshes and wood-lands. The protected nesting grounds for herons and other waterfowl are off-limits.

Richmondtown Restoration
A restored colonial village on Staten Island. The village includes the 1695 Voorlezer's House, the oldest schoolhouse in the United States. Visitors can watch demonstrations of colonial cooking, spinning, printing, and crafts.

FAST FACTS

POPULATION:

City: 7,322,564

Greater Metropolitan Area: 19,549,649

The Greater Metropolitan Area includes parts of New York State, New Jersey, Connecticut, and Pennsylvania.

AREA 368 square miles

CLIMATE New York City has a temperate climate, with hot, humid summers and cold, snowy winters. January temperatures average around 33 degrees Fahrenheit. The average July temperature is 70 degrees Fahrenheit. The city receives 44 inches of precipitation a year in the form of rain, sleet, and snow.

GOVERNMENT New York City has a mayor-council form of government. The mayor, the City Council president, and the 51 council members are all elected to 4-year terms. Each of the five boroughs elects its own president, who serves as an advisor to the mayor and City Council.

ECONOMY New York is a leading manufacturer of clothing, processed foods, furniture, light machinery, and electrical equipment. Much of the nation's publishing industry is based in the city. The Port of New York is a major center for the import and export of goods. Banking, insurance, and the sale of stocks and bonds are also major industries.

CHRONOLOGY

1609
Henry Hudson is the first European to see the Hudson River; he claims the river and the surrounding land for the Netherlands.

1625
Peter Minuit buys Manhattan from the Algonquian Indians; he establishes the Dutch settlement of New Amsterdam at the southern tip of the island.

1646
The first people of African descent are brought to New York as slaves.

1664
New Amsterdam surrrenders to a British fleet; the British rename the settlement New York.

1776
British troops capture New York City.

1783
The British leave New York.

1785
New York serves as the temporary U.S. capital.

1820
New York becomes the nation's biggest city, with 120,000 people.

1876
Central Park officially opens to the public.

1883
The Brooklyn Bridge is completed and nicknamed the "Eighth Wonder of the World."

1886
The Statue of Liberty is dedicated, a gift from France to the United States.

A view of the Dakota apartment building from Central Park

1892
Ellis Island opens as a station for processing millions of European immigrants.

1898
The five boroughs are united to form New York City, with a population of more than 3 million.

1927
The Holland Tunnel beneath the Hudson River links Manhattan with New Jersey.

1929
A crash in prices on Wall Street triggers a worldwide economic depression.

1931
The Empire State Building becomes the world's highest structure, 102 stories tall; the George Washington Bridge across the Hudson is completed.

1936
The Triborough Bridge links Manhattan, the Bronx, and Queens.

1952
The United Nations opens its headquarters in New York City.

1973
At 110 stories, the World Trade Center briefly becomes the world's tallest structure.

1989
David Dinkins becomes New York City's first African American mayor.

1993
A terrorist bomb explodes at the World Trade Center; a plot to bomb the UN Building and the Holland and Lincoln tunnels is uncovered.

NEW YORK CITY

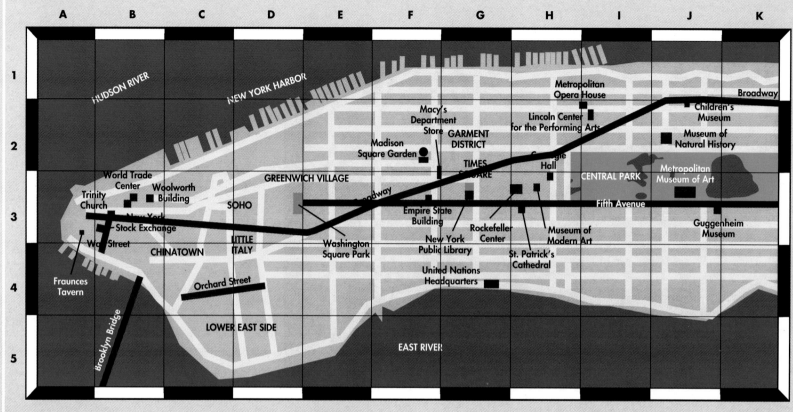

SURROUNDINGS

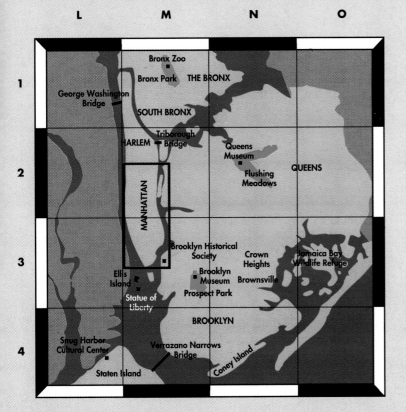

GLOSSARY

asset: Valuable resource

brusque: Abrupt, harsh

characters: Symbols that stand for words or syllables

enclave: Small enclosed community

indifference: Uncaring attitude

kimono: Long Japanese garment fastened at the waist with a wide sash

lofty: High, towering

monitor: To observe closely, keep watch

obelisk: Tall, tapered 4-sided stone pillar with a pyramid-shaped cap

orthodox: Following a strict set of rules or beliefs

outpost: Remote settlement

pinnacle: Peak, high point

quarter: To give lodging to

sari: Loose, graceful dress worn by Indian women

skirmish: Small battle

vendor: Seller

Picture Identifications

Cover: The "Big Apple"; the Statue of Liberty; New York schoolgirls; Central Park
Page 1: Children in Chinatown
Pages 4-5: The Manhattan skyline and the Hudson River
Pages 8-9: A Park Avenue traffic jam
Pages 22-23: An 1820 painting of New York as seen from New Jersey
Pages 32-33: Young women dressed like Betsy Ross for the Macy's Thanksgiving Day Parade
Pages 44-45: Children playing in a Central Park playlot

INDEX

Page numbers in boldface type indicate illustrations

ABOUT THE AUTHOR

Deborah Kent grew up in Little Falls, New Jersey, about forty minutes from Times Square. She received her bachelor of arts degree from Oberlin College, and earned a master's degree from Smith College School for Social Work. For four years, she worked at the University Settlement House on Manhattan's Lower East Side.

Ms. Kent wrote her first young-adult novel, *Belonging*, while living in San Miguel de Allende, Mexico. She has written more than a dozen novels, as well as numerous nonfiction books for young people. Though she has lived in many places, she still considers New York to be her city. She says no place else offers such possibilities.

Deborah Kent lives in Chicago with her husband and their daughter Janna.